BUILDING FROG FRIENDLY GARDENS

A practical guide to encouraging frogs
to visit and breed in gardens of
southwest Western Australia

By

KEN APLIN, ANTHEA PAINO AND LYNDAL SLEEP

Alcoa Frog Watch
The Western Australian Museum

ISBN 0 7307 5782 X

First Published 2000
Reprinted 2001
Reprinted May 2002

Cover designed by Hollis Rundle
Printed by Lamb Print, Perth, Western Australia

Published by the Western Australian Museum
Perth Cultural Centre, Francis Street, Perth, Western Australia 6000

CONTENTS

Overleaf: A Slender Tree Frog
alert for a passing meal.

PREFACE

As Coordinator of *Alcoa Frog Watch* since 1995 I have had the privilege of speaking to many thousands of Western Australians about their interests and experiences with frogs. Many of these conversations have been quite enlightening, some highly entertaining, and a few quite mind boggling! But almost all have contained either one or both of the following two elements.

The first is an obvious joy and delight on the part of virtually everybody who has had any personal contact with frogs. Why frogs are so popular is still intriguing to me. Perhaps it is just that frogs are so obviously harmless and vulnerable. Or perhaps it is because many people have had some personal contact with frogs, even if it has been a fleeting one. Almost everyone has a personal story about frogs.

Unfortunately, the second element is an acute awareness on the part of many people that frog numbers in both the metropolitan and the rural areas have declined over the last few decades. Most tragically, this means that many young people, especially those growing up in Perth, have rarely, if ever seen a frog, other than on the television or in glossy advertising.

Frogs are declining world-wide for many different reasons. In the southwest of Western Australia, the main reasons for the declines are probably

- continued destruction of frog habitat for agricultural, industrial and suburban use

- increased usage of environmental chemicals both in agriculture and domestic life

- the presence over the last 10-15 years of an exotic frog disease, caused by the parasitic skin fungus *Batrachochytrium* (an up-to-date summary of what we do and don't know about this disease has been included with this booklet for your reference)

Unless we start to counter these destructive forces, our southwestern frogs will almost certainly continue to decline and some may ultimately disappear altogether.

Three southwestern frogs are currently listed as Threatened Fauna. Each of these is found in a small area of the southern forest, and each is the subject of a special recovery

Plan by the Department of Conservation and Land Management and The Natural Heritage Trust. With all this help – and a little luck – these species may survive.

But what about all of the other frog species, the ones that in the past were super-abundant and occurred virtually everywhere through the region? Day by day the natural breeding, feeding and sheltering sites of these species are being degraded and destroyed. Day by day their populations are getting smaller and more fragmented.

How long can we afford to sit back and watch this trend continue? Should we wait until these species also qualify as critically endangered before we start to act? Personally, I don't think that we should.

Alcoa Frog Watch's *Building Frog Friendly Gardens* is a program with one simple goal – to get frogs back into peoples' gardens and thus back into their lives. I believe that, given a chance to plead their own case, frogs may well do the best job of convincing us to take greater care of the environment. I invite you to encourage them into your garden, and to listen to what they have to say.

Dr Ken Aplin

Alcoa Frog Watch Coordinator, 3rd November 2000

ACKNOWLEDGEMENTS

A great many people have contributed in different ways to the production of this booklet. Foremost among them are the many thousands of Alcoa Frog Watch members who have given their time to frogs and have shared their froggy experiences with us. This booklet is largely a result of their efforts. Special thanks go to Alcoa Frog Watch members Vivienne Elanta, Laurie Maddison and Kevin McKenzie, each of whom has shared their extensive practical knowledge of breeding local species. Johnny Prefumo of Ecosytems Environmental Consultants also shared his considerable experience in the business of 'frogscaping'.

We would also like to give special thanks to Suzanne Johnson of Alcoa World Alumina Australia for her unflagging support and enthusiasm for the Alcoa Frog Watch program, and to Kimlarn Frecker of the Western Australian Museum Foundation for her assistance with promotion and management of the program. Others at the Museum who have made invaluable contributions over the life of Alcoa Frog Watch are Mark Cowan, Ann Ousey, Greg Jackson, Vince McInerney, Malcolm Parker, Carolyn Mutzig, Di Davies, Lynne Broomhill, and Cassandra Landre.

Dale Roberts of the Department of Zoology, University of Western Australia, has generously allowed use of his recordings of frog calls within the Alcoa Frog Watch program. The following people gave permission to use photographs: Mark Cowan, Greg Harold, Brad Maryan, Harry de Jong and Liz Marcus.

Perry Lakes, Wembley – a major frog breeding site, nestled among well-established suburbs.

Herdsman Lake, Floreat Waters estate – frog habitats lost in the presumed interests of nearby residents. But is this really what people want?

CHAPTER 1:

INTRODUCTION

When did you last see a frog in your own garden?

Sadly, for many people, the answer will be 'not for many years' .. or perhaps, 'never'.

It does not have to be this way. If enough people in the community are willing to make small changes to their home gardens, frogs can be brought back into the suburbs and into our daily lives.

Just imagine

- the pleasure of watching frogs coming out to feed on a warm evening
- the excitement of hearing the first chorus of the breeding season
- the satisfaction of finding newly-laid frog spawn in your garden pond
- the wonder of sharing with children or grandchildren the miracle of tadpoles gradually changing into tiny frogs.

To be part of *Building Frog Friendly Gardens* all you need to make a start is a small garden or courtyard and a little spare time to read this booklet. By following our simple instructions, and with only a small investment of time and money, you will be able to start transforming your garden into a 'frog-friendly' one.

For people with cats and dogs – don't despair! As shall be explained later in this booklet, pets and frogs usually get along just fine.

Getting frogs back into our lives – in four easy steps

To help bring frogs back into your life, you will need to follow these four steps:

STEP 1: *Think like a frog*

If you were a frog, what would you be looking for in a suburban garden? To answer this question, you will need to understand a little bit about what it means to be a frog.

- What do frogs eat and drink?
- Where do frogs spend their time?
- What do frogs need in order to breed?

In the next two chapters we will provide answers to these and some other frequently asked questions, and introduce you to some of the fascinating frogs that you can expect to meet in your *Frog Friendly Garden*.

STEP 2: *Decide how you can help*

Once you have learned a little more about frogs, it is then time to decide on just what you can do to help.

- Would you just like to make your garden a safe haven for an occasional visiting frog?
- Or would you like to encourage frogs to breed in your garden?
- And if so, which species would you like to encourage?

It is of course quite possible to take one hop at a time – start with building a safe haven, then install a pond at a later date, when time or circumstances permit.

STEP 3: *Design your frog friendly garden*

Designing your garden requires some careful thought, but it can be great fun. In Chapter 4 we discuss some of the major issues in designing a Frog Friendly Garden.

These include

- Choosing plants that provide good frog habitat

- How to provide adequate food and shelter

- Where to place ponds to minimise maintenance and encourage breeding

From there, it's really a matter of using your imagination, your ingenuity and even your sense of humour. There are many different ways to accomplish the same result, and plenty of room to experiment. And lots of excellent ideas can be turned in reality with very simple materials and a minimum of effort.

STEP 4: *Get to work and enjoy it!*

In Chapters 5 and 6 we give step by step instructions on how to build or install a garden pond or bog garden, and how to go about establishing a healthy pond community including frogs, fishes and aquatic invertebrates.

In the last chapter of the booklet we provide some instructions on how to care for eggs and tadpoles, and for juvenile frogs as they emerge from your pond. We also provide some hints on caring for any sick or injured frogs that you might come across from time to time.

Tadpoling – an age-old and ageless pleasure.

CHAPTER 2:

A FROG'S EYE VIEW OF THE WORLD

Fortunately, its not so hard to think like a frog, or to see the world through a frog's eyes. This is because their basic needs are pretty much the same in all species of frogs, and also fairly similar to our own.

Like us, frogs need to breathe, drink and eat, and they need shelter from extremes of climate. Unlike us, frogs also need protection from a multitude of predators (although this would be different if we lived in many other parts of the world – just think lion or tiger!).

Drinking and breathing are actually more closely linked in frogs than they are in humans. Frogs do not seem to drink in any conventional sense, but instead take all of their water needs either through the skin or as part of juicy prey items. Frogs also breathe mainly through their skin. They do have lungs, but these are of fairly simple design and are just as important for puffing the body up in self-defense as in breathing. Importantly, their skin is only able to breathe if it is moist - hence the link.

This need to stay moist means that frogs will only be able to shelter in your garden if it contains sufficient moisture. This doesn't mean that it has to be wet underfoot. In the past local frogs have had to survive through numerous hot, dry summers and they have become extremely good at finding and using moisture. Different frog species developed different ways of doing this, some by burrowing into the soil or by getting under a rock or log, and others by nestling into the base of a dense plant where the air is kept slightly moist by water loss from the stems and leaves. For a garden to be too dry for frogs, it would really have to be a sun-baked desert, and even then it can be made 'frog-friendly' with a little bit of work.

Eating is what frogs like best. And, unlike Pooh Bear's friend Tigger, frogs really do eat everything. Well, almost everything. The only conditions are that it has to be moving, not too big, not too hard, and not too hairy!

Frogs hunt mainly by sight and are not very good at recognising shapes. For them to identify potential prey, they generally need to be sitting still, and the prey, moving.

A magnificent Hooting Frog in search of prey.

Then watch out! A lunge forward and a flick of the tongue later, and the food is in the mouth. Provided it's not too hairy or too large to swallow in one piece, then down the hatch it goes, often assisted by a downward push from the eyeballs that disappear into the eye-sockets in a most disconcerting fashion. Frogs have weak jaws with tiny or no teeth, and are unable to chew or break up their prey.

Larger frogs do not seem to mind eating smaller frogs and under some circumstances, will even eat members of their own species. Motorbike Frogs can be especially cannibalistic.

Only one local has a more specialised diet – the bizarre Turtle Frog which lives in dry, sandy soils and only seems to eat termites. What a champion!

Shelter is especially important for frogs. As explained above, this is mainly to protect their skin from extremes of heat and dryness. However, they also need shelter from predators ... of which there are many.

Around a natural wetland, frogs are eaten by just about everything, including water rats, lizards, snakes and turtles, numerous waterbirds such as swamp hens and ibises, and a range of bushland residents including ravens and bandicoots. The smaller frogs are even eaten by various invertebrates such as spiders, scorpions, centipedes and beetles. This makes frogs very important for the wider ecosystem, but for many individual frogs, it means that life is short and sweet!

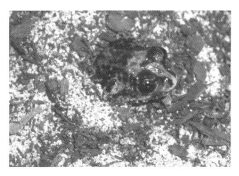

A Moaning Frog works its way backwards into the ground in search of moisture.

In a garden, frogs may be a bit safer than they are in a natural wetland. But as frog numbers increase, so too may the frequency of visits by hungry predators such as ibises and ravens. By providing frogs with plenty of shelter, you can at least give them a good chance of surviving these visits, but there is of course no guarantee. For this reason, we sometimes warn people not to get too attached to any individual frog, but rather to enjoy the population as a whole.

Garden frogs often face three new predators – cats, dogs and black rats. The first two of these do take a certain toll on garden frogs. However, in our experience it is often only a cat or dog's first encounter with a frog that leads to a sad end. This is because many of our local frogs contain mild toxins in their skin that can cause vomiting and convulsions in cats and dogs, and presumably taste horrible too. Most pets don't seem to go beyond the tasting stage, and the few that do will soon learn to leave frogs alone. However, we have heard of a few dogs that take delight in digging up and carrying frogs around, apparently without really harming them. Unusual behaviours of this kind are fortunately the exception rather than the norm. At any rate, the hopping proof is the fact that many Alcoa Frog Watch members have cats and dogs as well as thriving populations of garden frogs.

Black rats probably pose a greater threat to garden frogs, as they are clever enough to remove the toxic skin before eating the body. They are also smaller and able to enter narrow refuges that might harbour frogs.

Black rats pose other risks to human safety and health, and can be reported to local government for eradication. They are unlikely to be attracted to your property solely because of your frogs, but probably because of an abundance of flowers, fruit or seeds. However, once established in your garden, they may well have an impact on frog numbers.

What constitutes good sheltering habitat differs a little between frog species. Several of the larger species are excellent diggers and like to disappear below ground, either into damp soil beneath thick leaf litter or around reticulation, or in a child's sandpit. The larger tree frogs often shelter in a woodpile, beneath a garden sleeper, or in or amongst pot plants that receive regular watering. The smaller species are unable to dig and are more likely to be found nestled in dense vegetation. They seem to especially like getting into dense tussock grass or a thick grass mat, where the air is kept slightly moist by water loss from the leaves and stems.

Most frogs are capable of staying in these sheltering places without feeding for weeks or even months. This means that they can disappear from view for long periods, then suddenly reappear. Of course, they may have also been off on a wander – but more of that in the next chapter. The height of summer is one period when most frogs will remain dormant. However this is not true hibernation, as they will come out for a feed if it rains. One local species, the much-loved Motorbike Frog, seems to become less active during the winter months, emerging only on warmer nights to feed.

Selecting plants for a frog-friendly garden

Many people ask whether they will have to use exclusively native plants to build a frog-friendly garden? The honest answer is no. Many people have constructed a frog-friendly garden using only exotic plants, and have had great success breeding two or more frog species in their 'non-native' pond.

Having said this, however, there is certainly a strong case to be made for the use of native or better still, 'local native' plants in your garden. ('Native plant' is a general term that often refers to species from anywhere in Australia. 'Local native' plants are indigenous to your neighbourhood.) One reason is the fact that local native plants have evolved to suit our dry summer conditions, and generally need far less water than the exotics and even most other 'natives'. Furthermore, they rarely if ever require any added fertilizer to grow.

By planting local native plants, you will also be more faithfully recreating the frogs' natural habitat. Local native plants are more likely to attract a wider variety of local insects and other invertebrates than exotics or non-local native plants. This will provide a larger range of food items for your frogs to choose from, and may also lead to faster breakdown of litter, thereby enriching the soil and helping to keep it moist.

Local native species are generally less aggressive and easier to maintain than many exotic or Eastern States plants. This is particularly important for aquatic vegetation. Many exotic water plants grow very rapidly and must be regularly culled to keep them from smothering a pond. Some of these species can also be spread by birds to larger water bodies, where they can cause serious problems.

The booklet titled 'Perth Plants', and the related series of information sheets issued by *Greening Western Australia,* provide an excellent overview of how to employ local native plants in a variety of garden contexts.

Breeding requirements

Just about everyone knows the basic lifecycle of a frog – from egg to tadpole before turning into a frog – with the early life spent entirely in water. In general terms, frogs will need a pond or some other container of standing water in which to breed.

Among our local frogs, all but one species lay their eggs in or near standing water (the exception is the ever peculiar Turtle Frog; see next chapter). Beyond this, however, each species has specific requirements in terms of water depth, temperature, presence of plants etc. Other factors will determine whether the tadpoles are likely to develop successfully, and others again that relate to the needs of the newly-emerged young frogs.

For some species, the requirements are very specific and possibly difficult to recreate in a garden. However, for the majority of species, there is no reason why the requirements cannot be met. Once again, the trick is to think like a frog, and then get working on providing the right conditions.

The specific breeding requirements of each species are described in the next chapter. Look upon some of them as a challenge!

Squelching Froglets in 'amplexus' position in shallow water; male is behind.

Before leaving the subject of breeding, it is perhaps worth reminding readers that frogs use external fertilization of eggs. That means that a male frog must be present when a female releases the eggs in order to douse them with sperm. This tricky maneuver is carried out in a position called 'amplexus', in which the male sits or floats behind the female, grasping her under the arms or around the waist. If there is no male present to fertilise the eggs, they will simply fail to develop.

The frog fungus disease

A separate Alcoa Frog Watch information sheet on the frog fungus disease is included with this booklet. We have done this because research into the frog fungus issue is progressing in huge leaps and bounds (no pun intended!). This means that what we might write in this booklet will be very quickly out of date and may even be quite misleading within a year or so. Nevertheless, some things about the fungus seem reasonably well-established and should pass the test of time. We have limited our coverage here to points of special interest for garden frog enthusiasts.

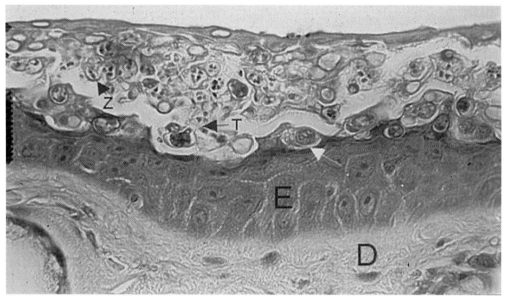

A thin section of frog skin infected with chytrid fungus. D = dermis; E = epidermis; T = discharge tube of infected cell; Z = infected cell containing zoospores. External surface of skin to top.

The frog fungus disease is caused by a microscopic water-borne fungus belonging to a group called the chytrid fungi. This particular chytrid fungus infects the outermost layer of the skin of juvenile and adult frogs, and can also infect the mouthparts of tadpoles. All species of frogs seem to be vulnerable to infection.

Infected tadpoles appear perfectly healthy in all other respects. Infected frogs can also appear quite healthy and may live for many months, or they can sicken and die within a period of a few days. Symptoms of the disease include lethargy, unusual or erratic behaviour, and an uncontrolled muscular twitching. Strangely, the skin itself shows no obvious signs of infection. The disease is spread by direct contact between frogs, or by a frog entering infected water. Around Perth it is active at all times of year, but particularly so during spring. At present there is no known cure for the disease.

The chytrid fungus appears to have been introduced into Western Australia in the mid-1980s. It has been present around Perth since 1989 and is now found in all of the major lakes and throughout the suburbs. It has been recorded in many garden frog populations.

What this means for frog lovers is that you must be prepared to face the possibility of a chytrid fungus outbreak in your area. If this does happen, you may observe some or all of the symptoms listed above and you might also find one or more dead frogs. However, it is unlikely that all of the frogs in your garden will die, and this should allow the population to build back up again with time. At present, we don't know whether surviving frogs have any acquired immunity or greater resistance to the disease.

If anyone does find a dead frog in their garden, it can be frozen and taken to the Western Australian Museum in the Cultural Centre, Perth, for testing. Diagnosis is a complex process that may take two or three months. The information gained will contribute greatly to our understanding of the frog fungus disease and its impact on local frogs.

CHAPTER 3:

MEET YOUR LOCAL FROGSTARS

There are 16 different species of frogs living within the wider Perth metropolitan region and 28 species found across the wider southwest region between Geraldton and Esperance. Some of these species are found in small areas only or in very specific habitats.

In most areas, you can expect to find between six and 10 species in natural wetland sites, with only three to four of these currently turning up regularly in suburban gardens. So it's not so difficult to work out which species are likely to come into your garden, nor is it too difficult to learn how to identify them or cater to their needs.

Here we will concentrate on the frog species that are most likely to enter or breed in suburban gardens. Anyone interested in learning more about the broader frog fauna should consider getting involved in the Alcoa Frog Watch *Neighbourhood Frog Monitoring* program. They can also consult the Museum's handbook titled *Frogs of Western Australia* by M. Tyler, L. A. Smith and R. E. Johnstone.

Frogs are easiest to identify from their breeding calls, some of which are unmistakable and unforgettable. Only males make the breeding call, which in some species doubles as a territorial or social call when made out of breeding season. In several species, there is a second type of call – a high pitched squealing made by members of both sexes when under threat, and known as a 'distress call'. A cassette of frog calls is available from Alcoa Frog Watch to help you to learn all of the different calls.

It is useful to distinguish three groups of frogs, both for easy identification and because members of each group share certain requirements. These are the tree frogs, the large ground frogs and the small ground frogs.

Motorbike Frog *(Litoria moorei)*

Tree Frogs

Tree frogs can be identified by the expanded, circular toe and finger pads that allow them to cling to smooth surfaces. Members of the two other groups have simple, pointed fingers and toes, and they are generally poor climbers.

There are two kinds of tree frogs found across the southwest region. Both quite commonly enter gardens, but the Motorbike Frog is seen far more frequently than any other local frog. The Slender Tree Frog is a smaller species that is probably heard more often than it is seen. Inland and east of Albany the Motorbike Frog is replaced by a close relative with very similar habits, the Spotted-thighed Frog, *Litoria cyclorhyncha*.

Motorbike Frogs (*Litoria moorei*) are large, versatile frogs that seem to thrive in artificial wetland habitats including suburban gardens. They grow to a maximum length of around 80 mm and seem equally at home on the ground or climbing in rushes or low trees. Motorbike Frogs probably take two years to reach breeding size and are known to live at least 8 years, perhaps considerably longer.

Motorbike Frogs are usually green or olive-brown, often with cream or golden striping or spots, and occasionally with black lines or spots. They have obvious, large toe-pads and lack any red or orange colouring on the inside of the thigh. Juveniles measure about 20mm and are usually more brightly patterned than the adults. Individuals of all ages are able to lighten or darken their colouring to match the background, but cannot change their basic patterning. Motorbike frogs often have distinctive patterning that allows individual frogs to be recognised over many years.

The call of the Motorbike Frog sounds remarkably like a motorbike changing gears! They usually call between August and January, but most eggs are laid during spring and early summer. About 1500-2000 eggs are laid in each clutch, the eggs spread over the surface of shallow water, either free floating or stuck to emergent vegetation. Motorbike Frogs are notoriously unselective about where they will lay their eggs, and the eggs have been found in swimming pools, bird baths, buckets of water, an old shoe. Anywhere!

Motorbike Frog tadpoles usually take 2 -3 months to develop, but sometimes this drags on much longer (see later section). In natural breeding sites, the newly emerged juveniles stay close to the water's edge until summer rainfall allows them to move off in search of shelter and food. Juveniles and adults can be quite adventurous, and often turn up many kilometres away from the nearest possible breeding site.

Slender Tree Frogs (*Litoria adelaidensis*) are delicate, acrobatic frogs that grow to around 60 mm in length. They have distinct toe pads, a pale stripe down the flank and highly distinctive red or orange spotting on the back of the thighs. Slender Tree Frogs can be either plain green or plain brown on their back, or occasionally a striped combination of the two. They can lighten or darken to match the background but cannot change their basic colouring.

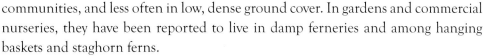

Around natural breeding sites, Slender Tree Frogs are usually seen perched among dense sedge or rush communities, and less often in low, dense ground cover. In gardens and commercial nurseries, they have been reported to live in damp ferneries and among hanging baskets and staghorn ferns.

The harsh 'grrrikk' call of the males can be heard from autumn through to mid-summer. However, eggs are laid only during late winter – early spring, at which time the frogs move down to water level and become difficult to find. The eggs are laid in clutches of a few hundred, attached to vegetation below water level.

Slender Tree Frog tadpoles take three months or more to develop, and seem to prefer areas of moderately deep water. Juveniles appear with the first autumn rains, so presumably emerge over the course of summer. Slender Tree Frogs are not as mobile or wide-ranging as Motorbike Frogs but they sometimes set off on a long trek between wetlands. Perhaps these stray individuals are the equivalent of our great explorers, or maybe they have been ostracized by their communities. There are some things that we may never know! On a more mundane level, we also don't know how long they take to reach breeding maturity, nor how long they live.

Large ground frogs

Three different groups of large ground frogs might turn up in your garden. All can grow to 60 mm or more, and all are very powerful diggers. Banjo Frogs and Moaning

Frogs are short-legged, fat-bodied frogs that have a prominent digging tubercle on the hind foot. Both of these groups are sometimes mistaken for Cane Toads, but they lack the strong bony ridges over the eyes that are the hallmark of a true toad.

Turtle Frogs are much more peculiar animals with a very fat body, a small rounded head and very stumpy limbs. Count yourself very lucky if you ever get to see one!

Banjo Frogs (*Limnodynastes dorsalis*) are easily distinguished from Moaning Frogs and their relatives by the presence of crimson markings in the groin and on the back legs. They usually have a yellow stripe running down the middle of the back and they grow to an adult size of 65-70 mm in length.

Banjo Frogs are among the hardiest and most adventurous of our local frogs and they often turn up many kilometres away from the nearest wetland habitat. What allows them to do this is the fact that they are powerful diggers, able to disappear a metre or more below ground in search of moisture. Like Motorbike Frogs, they can probably live for many years, provided they do not get eaten in the meantime!

The breeding call of a Banjo Frog is a loud, explosive 'bonk' which can be heard several kilometres away, especially at night. Many males often call in rapid succession, each trying to outdo the others for female interest, and the combined sound that they make is just like the sound of random banjo picking. Listen to them long enough and perhaps one day you will be rewarded by a few bars of the theme music from *Deliverance*!

Banjo Frog calling usually starts in mid-to-late winter and continues through to early summer. A mating pair produce a floating 'foam-raft' with the consistency of egg-white and containing upwards of 5000 eggs. These rafts can be found at any time through the calling period, but are most often seen during late winter and spring. Banjo Frog tadpoles develop very slowly, perhaps over 4-8 months, with the majority of juveniles emerging over summer. Summer and early autumn rains often trigger off mass movements of many hundreds or thousands of 20-30 mm long juvenile Banjo Frogs.

Although Banjo Frogs are quite often seen in gardens, they generally seem to return to their major breeding sites to call. However, there are some records of them calling from suburban garden ponds, and one record of egg masses laid in a large pond at a suburban Perth school.

Moaning Frogs (*Heleioporus eyrei*) are the best known of a group of five burrowing frog species. These all have very similar lifestyles, but differ in appearance and in the male breeding calls.

The Moaning Frog itself is found throughout the Perth region, extending into the Darling Range and through the forested country to the south coast. It is a short-legged, round-bodied frog with prominent, bulging eyes. Juveniles measure around 10 mm in length, and both sexes grow to around 65 mm. Adults can live for many years, but the average age of breeding adults is probably 3-4 years old.

Moaning Frogs can suffer extreme dehydration while they forage on a hot summers night, then regain the body moisture during the day by burrowing deep into the soil. In this way they are able to remain active, even through the hottest months of the year.

The breeding season for Moaning Frogs starts with the first autumn rains. At this time, Moaning Frogs can be seen moving *en masse* towards their traditional breeding sites. Males dig a breeding burrow in a position that they expect to be under water later in the season. They then start to make their mournful 'whooo whooo' call from just inside the burrow, calling from dusk to dawn in the pursuit of love. If a female enters the burrow, the pair will lay a foamy egg mass at the base of the burrow. The tadpoles hatch and start to develop in the burrow, and are usually flushed into the adjacent wetland a few weeks to one month later. Tadpole growth is usually completed within another month or so, with juveniles coming out around the margins of the wetland in late winter or early spring. The juveniles probably remain close to the wetlands for a further 2-3 months, before moving off into bushland or suburbia under cover of a warm, wet early summer's night. Outside of the brief breeding season, the majority of adult moaning frogs can be found far away from the breeding sites.

In areas where the original wetlands have been destroyed, Moaning Frogs now try to breed in gardens, often to the distress of the inhabitants. In many cases, these 'garden moaners' probably do not manage to attract a female into the burrow. And even if they do, the tadpoles laid in these burrows are trapped and will presumably die without help. The future of these suburban populations is thus very much in the hands of individual householders (see p. 61 instructions on how to help).

The remaining four members of the Moaning Frog group are found mainly in forested areas in the Darling Range and southern forests. Two species are occasionally reported from gardens in the hills suburbs of Perth. These are the Chocolate Spotted Frog (*Heleioporus albopunctatus*) and the Hooting Frog (*Heleioporus barycragus*), both of which tend to dig their burrows in harder clay soils along streams. One of the other species, the aptly-named Whooping Frog, makes a loud 'whoop whoop whoop' that puts the gentle 'whoo who' of the Moaning Frog to shame for volume and sheer irritation value. Breeding sites of the Whooping Frog are mostly quite remote from human habitation – probably because any people long ago moved on! (If you don't believe this, listen to an Alcoa Frog Watch cassette tape).

Turtle Frogs (*Myobatrachus gouldii*) are equally bizarre in both appearance and habits. They are the only local frog to have a specialised diet – consisting solely of termites, and one of only two Australian frog species that burrow head-first rather than using the more usual reversing-in technique.

Turtle Frogs are also unusual in having done away with a free-swimming tadpole stage of development – the young frogs hatching straight from large eggs that are deposited at the base of a deep breeding burrow. The 'aarrk aarrrkk' call of Turtle Frogs can be heard on rainy nights in late spring to early summer, usually coming from the highest points in the landscape. Baby Turtle Frogs are first seen in early winter and measure only 10-12 mm. It is not known how long they take to mature, nor how long they can live.

Turtle Frogs are still fairly common in certain bushland areas around Perth. However, with continued clearance of their preferred Banksia woodland habitat, the future survival of Turtle Frogs in many areas may depend on their ability to live and breed in gardens.

Small ground frogs

Five species of small ground frogs are found through all or part of the southwest region. They are all less than 50 mm in length and are generally poor diggers. All of them have been known to live and breed in gardens, although many people are not even aware that they are there! However, despite their small size, all of them may be able to live for 5-10 years.

Squelching Froglets and **Bleating Froglets** (*Crinia insignifera* and *Crinia pseudinsignifera*) are two closely related species, the first found on the Swan Coastal Plain and the second in the Darling Range and further inland and south. They differ mainly in their call, which is a high-pitched 'rrriicck rricckk' in the Squelching Froglet and a quavering 'baaaa-baaaa' in the Bleating Froglet.

Both are small, delicately built frogs, with adult females growing no larger than 30 mm in length (males slightly smaller). They are unable to burrow into soil but are often found sheltering under logs or deep inside tussocks of grass.

Males call through winter and into early spring, but calling activity becomes most intense in mid-winter when females are ready to lay eggs. Clutches of a few hundreds of eggs are laid onto a silty or sandy bottom in shallow, open water. The tadpoles remain in shallow water and take several months to develop. Juveniles are about 8 mm long and are usually found close to the water's edge.

Clicking Froglets (*Crinia glauerti*) are the smallest of our local frogs, with adult females growing to 24 mm (males are slightly smaller). They are usually found in dense ground cover under shrubs or trees, often in areas prone to seasonal flooding. Clicking Froglets have a patchy

distribution among the wetlands of the Swan Coastal Plain, and are often found in combination with either of the previous two species. Clicking Frogs have more intense black markings on their belly, often combined with a faint 'crucifix' made up of a line running down the centre of the belly and a cross-piece running across the chest.

Males can be heard calling at almost any time of year, but get really serious about it from late winter to early spring when the females are carrying eggs. Small clutches of eggs are laid in shallow water, and even in small depressions with only 1-2 cm of water. The tadpoles take 2-3 months to develop.

Quacking Frogs (*Crinia georgiana*) sound remarkably like ducks talking in their sleep – five or six distinct 'quack's, repeated quickly. They are widespread and common through much of the southwest but are found only along the major rivers and brooks on the Swan Coastal Plain. They grow to around 40 mm in length and can be distinguished from the other small ground frogs by the presence of crimson markings in the groin and on the back legs.

Adult Quacking Frogs are often confused with young Banjo Frogs, the two species both having crimson in the groin. They are most easily distinguished by looking at the hind foot – Banjo Frogs have a prominent digging tubercle that looks almost like a sixth toe. Another giveaway is that Quacking Frogs have a crimson or golden-coloured upper eyelid.

Quacking Frogs call through winter and spring and lay clutches of a few hundred eggs in shallow pools or on moist soil or mossy rocks. The tadpoles develop quickly and turn into tiny, jet-black juveniles measuring only 5-7 mm. Newly-emerged juvenile Quacking Frogs look for all the world like tiny crickets as they hop around underfoot.

Lea's Frog (*Geocrinia leai*) is found throughout the forested parts of the southwest and also on the southern Swan Coastal Plain around Bunbury and Busselton. They grow to around 35 mm in length and are distinguished from the other small ground frogs by their smooth greenish belly and small but discernible toe pads. The call is a distinct 'chic chic', heard through winter and usually coming from dense stands of broad-leafed sedges growing in or alongside deep water. Lea's Frog calls around garden ponds in the Perth hills suburbs, but we don't know for sure whether they breed in such places.

Lea's Frog has the unusual habit of suspending its egg mass in vegetation hanging above still or flowing water. Several females seem to lay their eggs in one spot, which is sometimes defended by a small but feisty male. The tadpoles develop in the hanging mass until they become too heavy, at which time they drop into the water below. The tadpoles take a further 4 months or so to complete their development.

Crawling Frogs (*Pseudophryne guentheri*) are small, toad-like creatures with short legs and warty skin. They crawl rather than hop and have a distinctive pattern of bold black and white markings on their belly. A related species, the Western Toadlet, occurs further inland. Both species are commonly found around granite outcrops, where they shelter under loose rock slabs and breed in temporary rock pools. Adults of both species reach around 40-50 mm, with females larger than males.

The low, harsh 'grrrrkk' call of male Crawling Frogs can be heard through winter, often from alongside streams. The males call from shallow breeding tunnels under leaf litter and often seem to attract several females, resulting in a network of egg-filled tunnels in the one area. The tadpoles hatch on land and must rely on heavy rains to wash them across the ground surface and into a stream. What a risky way to start out in life!

Around Perth, Crawling Frogs are found only on the harder, clay-rich soils along the major rivers and brooks. In the hills they are found on gravelly, lateritic soils.

CHAPTER 4:

PLANNING YOUR FROG FRIENDLY GARDEN

Now that we have you thinking like a frog and have introduced you to some of your future frog friends, it is time to move on to the 'doing' bits – planning and then, action!

The first step in planning is to decide what type of frog-friendly garden is best for you. Would you like frogs to just visit or live in your garden on a seasonal basis, perhaps as they move to and from their seasonal breeding ground? Or would you like one or more species of frogs to actually breed in your garden?

Both types of garden will play an important role in conserving your local frog fauna. And there is of course the option of taking one hop at a time – start with a safe haven, then install a breeding pond later, when time or circumstances permit.

In making this decision you may need to give some thought to some or all of the following issues:

- Will the sound of frogs calling be disruptive to your family or neighbours? There are various ways of reducing the risk of losing friends, but it may be difficult to eliminate the noise entirely.

- Are your family or neighbours concerned about a possible increase in mosquitoes if you install a garden pond? If so, you may need to explain to them how you intend to control mosquitoes – and be prepared to take extra action if they feel that mosquito numbers have increased.

- How large a garden area do you have, and what other areas are available for use by your frogs? Remember that some frogs can be quite prolific breeders and excess juveniles may well try to colonise surrounding areas.

- Are you prepared to make a long-term commitment to the frogs? Remember that most of our local frogs probably live for 5-10 years, perhaps even longer, and that by installing a pond you will almost certainly bring about an increase in local frog numbers. The offspring will need places to feed and shelter in coming years.

The next step is to decide whether or not to try to encourage any particular kinds of frogs. As explained in the previous chapter, Motorbike Frogs are not only found just about everywhere through the southwest, but will also breed in just about any standing body of water. They will probably move into your frog-friendly garden no matter what. However, most of the other species are a bit fussier about where they like to live and breed, and some are only found in certain areas or certain kinds of habitat. These may take some more careful planning, especially if you would like them to breed in your garden.

What frogs can you expect to see in your garden?

The following lists will give you a pretty good idea of which frog species you can expect to see in or around your garden in various parts of the southwest. For areas not included here, or for more detailed advice, you can contact Alcoa Frog Watch staff at the Western Australian Museum.

NORTHERN SWAN COASTAL PLAIN
(CERVANTES TO MANDURAH)

Motorbike Frog
Slender Tree Frog
Banjo Frog
Moaning Frog
Squelching Froglet
Clicking Froglet
Turtle Frog
Quacking Frog (inland and along main watercourses)

SOUTHERN SWAN COASTAL PLAIN
(PINJARRA TO DUNSBOROUGH)

Motorbike Frog
Slender Tree Frog
Banjo Frog
Moaning Frog
Squelching Froglet
Clicking Froglet
Lea's Frog
Quacking Frog (inland only)
Crawling Frog (inland only)

MARGARET RIVER AREA

Motorbike Frog
Slender Tree Frog
Banjo Frog
Moaning Frog
Bleating Froglet
Clicking Froglet
Quacking Frog
Lea's Frog

ALBANY AREA

Motorbike Frog
Slender Tree Frog
Banjo Frog
Moaning Frog
Bleating Froglet
Clicking Froglet
Quacking Frog
Lea's Frog

DARLING RANGE	GERALDTON AREA
Motorbike Frog	Motorbike Frog
Slender Tree Frog	Slender Tree Frog
Banjo Frog	Banjo Frog
Moaning Frog	Moaning Frog
Chocolate Spotted Frog	Bleating Froglet
Hooting Frog	Crawling Frog (inland localities)
Bleating Froglet	Turtle Frog
Clicking Froglet	Humming Frog
Quacking Frog	
Lea's Frog	
Crawling Frog	

Creating a safe haven for frogs

A safe haven for visiting frogs needs to provide plenty of shelter and an abundance and variety of food. It may also need to provide some protection against predators.

Sheltering places can be designed to suit one kind of frog alone; or they can be made more diverse to accommodate all possible froggy visitors, including tree frogs and the various large and small ground frogs.

A good starting point for all frogs is to think of ways to retain as much soil moisture as possible in your garden, especially over summer. Allow leaf litter to accumulate in shady areas of the garden. Leaf litter acts as a physical barrier to water loss and also breaks down over time to increase the organic content and moisture holding properties of the soil. These litter beds will also act as the 'food factory' for your garden (see below).

If your garden does not produce much natural litter, then a good alternative is to purchase some organic mulch from a garden or soil centre. Some of this can be mixed with the surface soil in a garden bed, but you should set aside enough to top it off with a 5-10 cm thick layer of solid mulch.

For larger frogs, shelter can be provided in numerous ways. Here are a few ideas to get you thinking:

- piles of loosely stacked bricks or tiles, perhaps covered by a layer of tree or leaf litter

- criss-crossed layers of railway sleepers or other old timber

- sections of old ceramic piping or PVC pipe, buried at an angle and with the entrance partially closed by a brick or tile

- logs or rocks (but please, not taken from a natural bushland area – tree loppings are fine)

- rolls of old, natural fibre carpet, buried under a thin layer of soil or litter

All sheltering places will be more inviting if they are positioned in shady positions in your garden, and even more so if they are placed close to potential sources of frog food. Piles of sleepers or logs placed in litter beds underneath shrubs are especially effective. If your garden is completely lacking in natural shade, then it may be worth investing in some shade cloth and suspending this over litter beds or other sheltering areas until such time as some trees or shrubs grow up. Shade cloth and other construction materials can often be picked up from road verges during 'council cleanup' periods.

The large ground frogs can be further encouraged into your garden by providing them with cool and damp areas in which to pass the summer months. One way to do this is to identify areas in the garden that tend to receive excess water over summer, such as alongside a garden tap or guttering downpipe. Dig out an area to a depth of half a metre or more, line it with any heavy duty plastic, and fill it back in. This will provide an area that retains moisture below ground even through the height of summer, and it may well attract passing Banjo or Moaning Frogs. A similar effect is sometimes

A Banjo Frog found sheltering under a log in a garden wood pile.

achieved accidentally when people build a garden sand pit for their kids. How many people remember digging up Banjo or Moaning Frogs while playing in the sandpit? Come on now, own up all you adults.

For the small ground frogs, tree branches and pieces of untreated timber can provide good shelter, especially if these are part-buried within a mature, moist litter-bed. However, to support large populations of these smaller species, it is probably necessary to plant some areas of dense ground cover plants. Tussock grasses and sedges like *Juncus* are probably best of all – around natural wetlands these often contain scores of tiny frogs tucked away safely in the centre of a big clump. As a simple stopgap measure while these plants get established, it may be sufficient to allow some of your lawn to remain unmown, perhaps against a fence or in an otherwise unused corner of the garden.

In a well-designed frog-friendly garden, it shouldn't be necessary to provide any direct watering, even over summer. Just remember, frogs were almost certainly living in the location now occupied by your garden, long before the garden hose or reticulation was invented!

An ideal 'frog-friendly' garden, providing shade, shelter and a breeding pond.

Providing food for frogs can be kept extremely simple or it can be turned into an elaborate science! Consider the notion of *carrying capacity*. The carrying capacity of your garden is basically the number of frogs that it can accommodate on an ongoing basis. This will be determined by various factors including the number of sheltering places. However, the single largest factor is undoubtedly the quantity of frog-friendly food.

As we saw earlier, frogs feed exclusively on live prey, which in effect means all of the 'creepy-crawlies' including spiders, beetles, moths, snails and slugs, slaters or woodlice, moths and flies. In general, the only rule is – the larger the frog, the larger the food items that it can eat.

The amount of frog food in your garden will be determined by many factors including its size, the diversity of plants, the quantities of litter and compost, the number and types of sheltering places and the nature of the surrounding areas. For example, a garden backing onto bushland will almost certainly have more invertebrate life than one surrounded by gardens with fence-to-fence concrete or lawns. The amount of food may also be determined by your use of chemicals such as pesticides and herbicides, many of which have both direct and indirect effects on invertebrate life.

There are various ways that you can increase the diversity and abundance of frog food in your garden:

- Plant a wide variety of different plants with differing growth and flowering periods. Native plants probably attract even more invertebrates than exotic plants, and have many other benefits including more efficient use of water and soil nutrients.

- Compost as much as possible of your kitchen waste.

- Avoid the use of chemicals in your garden. The vast majority of these are almost certainly harmful to frogs and their prey (even those that claim not to be). Frogs are actually a very effective means of controlling many garden pests, including slugs and snails, and slaters.

- Don't allow garden cuttings to go to waste; cut them up and add them to compost or leaf litter. Try to recycle all organic matter in your garden.

Even the most spectacularly frog friendly garden must eventually run out of naturally occurring frog food. Should you wish to support even larger numbers of frogs, then you will have to contemplate the option of supplementary feeding. There are various things that you can try:

- Place garden lights low to the ground and alongside the frog sheltering areas. These will attract extra flying insects from far and wide.

- Set aside an area for disposal of fruit peel and rotten fruit. Small flies and other flying invertebrates will probably come swarming in.

- Construct specific frog feeding stations to provide supplementary food. Frogs will soon learn to come to the station for food. One possible design, based on a self-perpetuating colony of mealworms, is shown in the Figure. You can also experiment with other kinds of colonies based on slaters, earwigs or crickets, perhaps using old newspapers or cardboard as food. The possibilities are almost endless, and you can have a lot of fun trying out your new and wild designs!

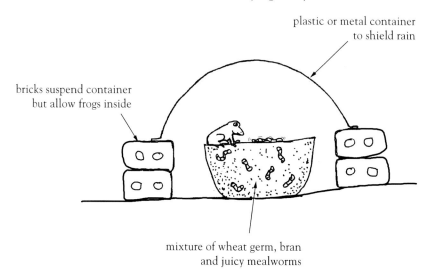

plastic or metal container to shield rain

bricks suspend container but allow frogs inside

mixture of wheat germ, bran and juicy mealworms

Control of predators may be necessary at certain times, especially when you only have a small numbers of frogs in your garden. However, in the longer term, visits from potential predators such as water birds and lizards should be viewed as a measure of your success in restoring the wider, suburban ecosystem.

One group of predators that most people would rather not see in their garden are snakes, especially the striped variety! Tiger Snakes do in fact feed mainly on frogs, and there are some concerns that frog ponds will encourage visits by these innocent but none-the-less dangerous predators. In reality, there is very little chance of this ever happening. A good test case is provided by the suburbs of Wembley and Churchlands in Perth, both of which abut directly against Tiger Snake-infested Herdsman Lake. Neither suburb has any problem with Tiger Snakes, despite the presence of many lush gardens with healthy frog populations. As a rule then, building a frog friendly garden is unlikely to ever result in problems with snakes, unless of course your garden backs straight into a swampy area already infested by these magnificent predators.

One way that you can give your frogs some extra protection is to enclose certain areas such as pond or litter bed under an open-mesh wire cage. Provided the mesh size is not too small, this won't stop frogs from coming and going, but it may well deter an ibis or a raven from wreaking havoc, especially at times when there are lots of young frogs moving around. Another possible defense would be to install bird deterrents such as are used to protect fruit trees. If anyone does build a giant, bird-frightening scarecrow with the face of a frog, we would like a photo for the next edition!

Allow frogs the freedom to move

One of the special problems that frogs face in a suburban environment is the sheer number of physical barriers to movement. These include the obvious things like roads, buildings and fences, but also the many vast tracts of low, fairly lifeless grassland that we call lawns and playing fields.

Some of these barriers are less of an obstacle to the climbing tree frogs than to the ground frogs, and some may appear much more formidable to a timid Clicking Froglet than to a swashbuckling Banjo Frog. Nevertheless, there is no doubt that many frogs simply lose their way in the maze of buildings and fences that we call home.

On a small scale, it might not be too difficult to allow frogs greater freedom of movement. Many people have observed Motorbike Frogs using the same perch or sheltering place in their garden for months or years on end. This shows clearly that they have a good sense of direction and location, and suggests that they would be clever enough to learn the location of any passages between adjacent gardens. In this light, it might be worth allowing passage through fences by cutting one or more small holes at ground level. These might give your frogs a larger feeding area and maybe a richer social life!

A logical extension of this idea would be to install frog passageways beneath some of the busier roads. Far too many frogs are killed on our metropolitan and semi-rural roads, especially on rainy nights. Okay, maybe this is a bit fanciful in the established suburbs, but is there any reason why these frog 'underpass' tunnels could not be incorporated into the design of new suburbs? They might be especially beneficial in areas where new roads are placed closed to wetlands or between wetlands and patches of remnant bushland. The tunnels might also save the lives of many reptiles, some of which are probably many decades old when they are flattened by an oblivious driver.

Frogs and swimming pools

How do frogs and a swimming pool mix in a garden? This frequently-asked question actually covers a couple of issues, for which there may not be easy solutions. We do know from many reports that frogs, especially Motorbike Frogs, will often lay their eggs in swimming pools (usually salt-water rather than chlorinated pools). We also know that many frogs also drown in swimming pools.

The problem with frog spawn usually seems to arise in gardens where the swimming pool is the only water body available for egg-laying and where the chlorine or salt level has been allowed to fall through winter. Two possible solutions come to mind. The first is to give the frogs some alternative water for egg-laying, whether in the form of an inviting pond or just some empty garbage bins or similar. The second is to also chlorinate or salt the pool at the first sound of a Motor-cross rally in the garden (that will be the frogs!). Perhaps used in combination, these two actions might result in the eggs being laid in a more convenient place next time around.

The second issue concerns the problem of accidental drownings of frogs in swimming pools. One practical step that can be taken here is to provide floating ramps to enable frogs to climb out on their own. This will probably save a fair number of Motorbike Frogs, but is unlikely to have much impact on the large ground frogs that may not be able to stay afloat long enough to locate the ramp. In these cases, the better solution is probably to keep those species out in the first place.

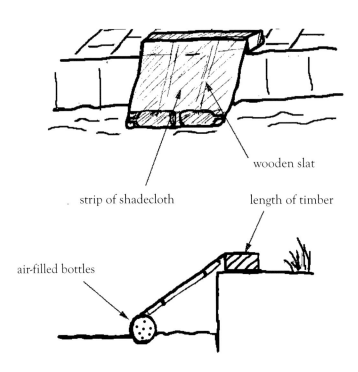

wooden slat

strip of shadecloth   length of timber

air-filled bottles

If the pool is raised slightly above ground, this may not be too difficult as the number of possible access points for the non-climbers may not be very high. Should it turn out that there are really only a few places for them to get through, then some effort could perhaps be made to limiting future frog access through these carriageways.

This scenario obviously doesn't work on a swimming pool that is sunken to ground level all the way around. In that case, more floating ramps is probably the only solution. Unless of course, the owner is prepared to go the full hog and convert the entire pool into a huge and magnificent bog garden!

Creating a breeding habitat for frogs

As you have probably gathered by now, creating a breeding habitat for frogs involves much more than just installing a pond, although this is obviously an important part of the process. In the next two chapters we will take you through each of the steps that are required for successful frog breeding in your garden, namely:

- Installing a pond or bog garden
- Establishing a pond ecosystem
- Caring for frog eggs and tadpoles
- Caring for juvenile frogs

Follow these steps and you may soon be enjoying your own, vibrant garden frog community!

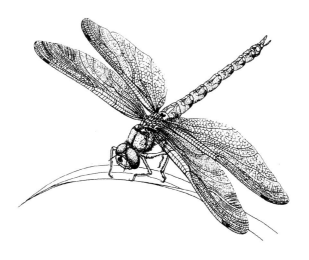

CHAPTER 5:

BUILDING A FROG POND

A pond can be a magnificent addition to a garden environment – a cool and tranquil haven where the world slips back to a time when silence was broken only by the gentle whir of a dragonfly's wings or by the plop of a diving frog. Alternatively, a garden pond can be a green, smelly embarrassment, devoid of any life and of any charm!

The difference between these scenarios is largely one of careful planning and design. And of understanding, which is why we will begin this chapter with a brief overview of a pond ecosystem.

The pond ecosystem

Ideally, your garden pond will be a self-sufficient, functioning ecosystem. This means that there will be a balance between all of the various chemical, physical and biological processes. The pond itself should be virtually maintenance-free and provide all of the basic needs for successful frog breeding.

In a healthy pond, much of the nutrients are bound up in the various primary producers (plants, algae) and in two food chains (see Figure on next page). One food chain involves **herbivores** such as water snails, water fleas and midge larvae, all of which feed on plants and algae. The other involves **detritovores** that feed on organic detritus derived from inwashing sediments and from the breakdown of dead plant and animal life. Detritovores include numerous aquatic worms, shrimps and yabbies, water boatmen, and the larvae of some beetles and caddisflies. Both of these food chains are topped off by a host of predators, including water boatmen and backswimmers, and the larvae of dragonflies, damselflies and water beetles. Higher predators that feed on all types of pond life include many kinds of water birds, and some larger predatory insects and spiders.

The primary role of tadpoles in a pond is as herbivores, browsing on aquatic plants and algae, although they also consume organic detritus. Frogs, as we know, are predators, although they are also consumed by numerous larger predators.

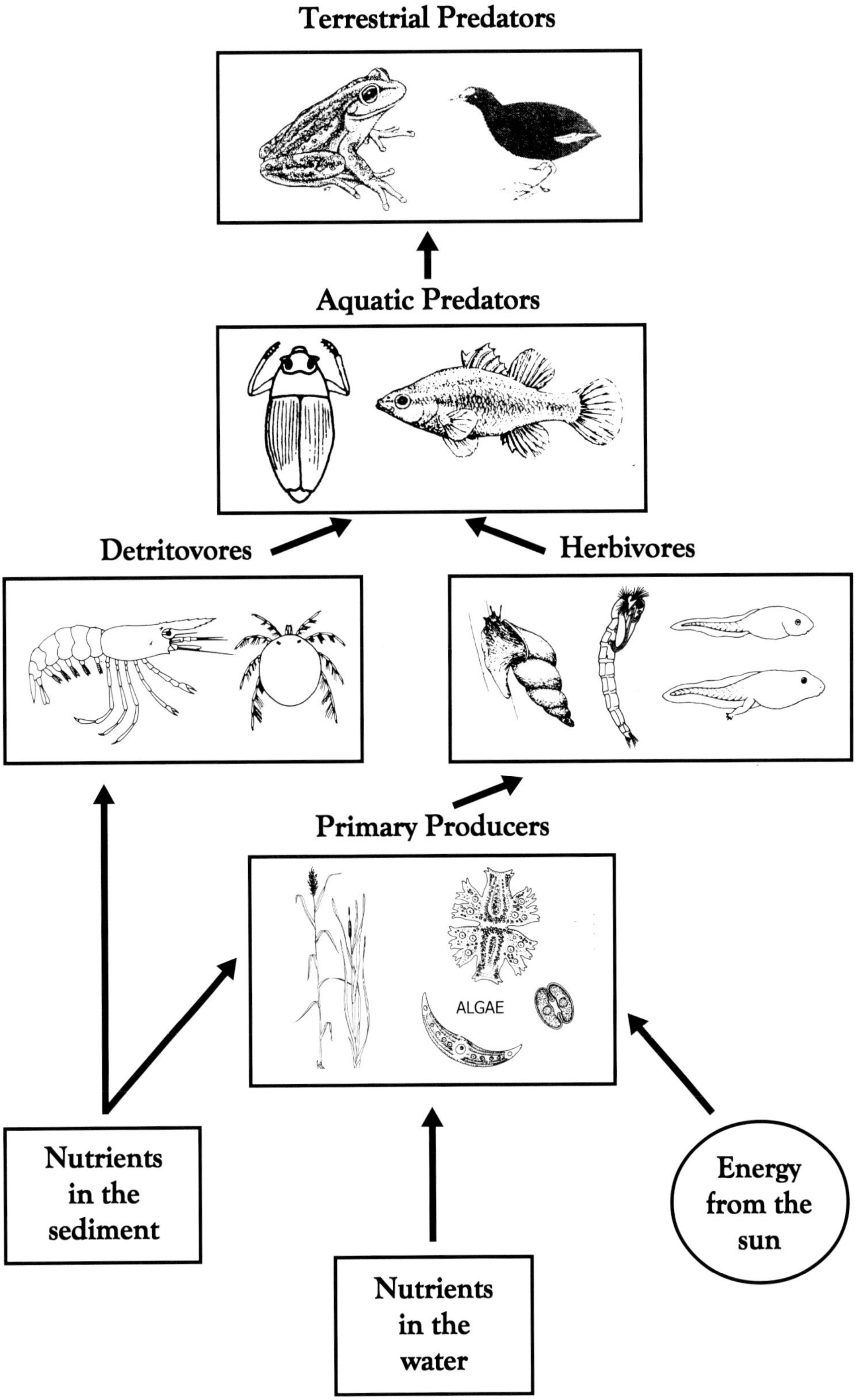

Terrestrial Predators

Aquatic Predators

Detritovores

Herbivores

Primary Producers

ALGAE

Nutrients
in the
sediment

Nutrients
in the
water

Energy
from the
sun

Water plants not only look attractive, they also play a vital role in maintaining the health of any pond. Their root systems remove nutrients from the water or bottom sediment, converting them into leaves and flowers that in turn feed a multitude of creatures. Their stems and leaves remove carbon dioxide from the water and air, and release life-supporting oxygen back into the water. Those plants with the bulk of their foliage underwater are the best oxygenators. Living and dead leaves provide shade and shelter, and a stage on which all manner of miniature life dramas are played out.

Excess nutrients pose the main threat to a healthy pond. This occurs when too much organic matter or fertilizer end up in the pond. Excess nutrient can make the water cloudy and can lead to rapid growth of algae and potentially harmful bacteria. This in turn leads to a decrease in the dissolved oxygen, and the release of harmful toxins into the water. The effect on pond life can be sudden and severe, with further threat of poisoning visiting waterbirds. The characteristic foul stench of algal blooms is known to many people who live close to the major wetlands in Perth, almost all of which are unable to deal with the huge quantities of inflowing nutrients. Algal blooms are also favoured by rising water temperatures, which makes them most prevalent over summer.

Mosquitoes can pose a serious health risk if they are allowed to breed up to large numbers. As a rule, mosquitoes prefer to breed in still, stagnant water rather than in moving or fresh water. In a healthy pond containing frogs and other wildlife, mosquitoes and their larvae are generally also kept under control as a result of predation by dragonflies and damselflies.

Where large numbers of mosquitoes are encountered in a garden, the problem is usually due to the presence of small bodies of stagnant water in bowls under pot plants or similar. In these circumstances, mosquitoes can be controlled quite simply by tidying up these small containers of stagnant water around a garden.

Several of the local native fish are quite good at reducing numbers of mosquito larvae (see p. 57). However, for added protection and peace of mind, it may be worth incorporating a circulating pump into your pond design. A pump will reduce the risk of your pond becoming stagnant and home to the telltale 'wrigglers'.

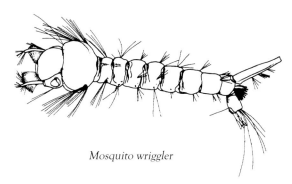

Mosquito wriggler

Pond placement

Many potential problems can be avoided by careful placement of your pond.

The most important thing is to get the correct balance between sun and shade for your pond. Ideally, at least one third of the pond surface should be sunlit through much of the day. Some sunlight is necessary to stimulate the healthy growth of plants, algae and aquatic invertebrates, but too much will result in overheating, loss of oxygen from the water, and possible algal blooms.

If you have no choice other than to locate your pond in full sun, you may still be able to obtain the desired level of shade through planting tall sedges, shrubs and edging plants near the pond. The addition of aquatic plants, especially those with large leaves (such as water lilies), can also give extra shade in the water itself. At a pinch, you might also consider using shade cloth or some other physical barrier, at least until your fringing plants reach the desired size. Water depth is another factor to consider here, as a shallow pool will heat up more rapidly than a pond that incorporates a deep well of cool water.

A second important consideration in pond placement is to avoid surface flow or seepage of water from any area of lawn or garden bed that has had fertiliser or compost applied, as this may upset the natural nutrient balance. The same applies for any area that has been treated with any kind of chemical, although in this case the outcome may be even more dire. Many aquatic creatures including frog eggs and tadpoles are extremely sensitive to these chemicals and to the surfactants or wetting agents with which they are commonly combined.

A third factor is the impact of natural leaf-fall from overhanging shrubs or trees. This can be quite difficult to judge in advance. A thin layer of leaves on the bottom of your pond is actually quite desirable, as it represents a source of nutrients and provides shelter for numerous pond creatures. However, if this layer becomes too thick, it may become anaerobic and start to draw oxygen from the water, turning it stagnant. In this event, you should scoop some of this material out of the pond and perhaps prune back some of the excess, overhanging foliage. If pruning is not possible, then a wire screen over the pool may be needed to catch some of the excess leaf-fall.

Some types of overhanging shrubs and trees should be avoided if at all possible. This includes most of the soft-leafed exotic trees, especially those that are deciduous. The leaves of these trees tend to decompose rapidly, leading to excess nutrient release and a loss of oxygen. Another group to avoid are plants that shed poisonous leaves or flowers, such as oleanders and pine trees. Leaf fall from these plants will probably kill many pond creatures including tadpoles and frogs. Your local nursery staff should be able to tell you whether any particular garden plant has poisonous leaves or flowers.

Another thing to consider is the placement of your pond relative to the various sheltering and feeding areas in your garden. Ideally, the pond or ponds should be located close to these areas, making it easy and safe for frogs to move from one to the other. This may be especially important for the smaller ground frogs, many of which are reluctant to cross any open ground.

Finally, it is worth giving some thought to the possible reaction that your frog chorus might draw from members of your family or your neighbours. Just be sure to remember that some of our local frogs (Slender Tree Frogs in particular) have a harsh, penetrating call that in magnificent full-throated chorus in the middle of the night can easily be mistaken for a hideous racket!

More seriously, there are some things that you can do to lessen the impact of a loud frog chorus. Apart from taking care to position your breeding pond as far as possible from potential critics, it may be possible to build or plant an effective barrier that should help to deflect and dissipate even the most penetrating chorus.

Pond design and construction

Designing a new pond can be great fun and is a tremendous opportunity to test your experimental prowess. For some frog species, design of an effective breeding pond can probably be looked upon as battle of wits and wills – human ingenuity and determination pitted against pure amphibian fickleness.

Before starting work on your pond design, you will need to answer these three questions:

- Which frog species are you going to try to breed in your pond?
- What raw materials do you intend using?
- Do you want to incorporate a pump?

Selection of frog species

Some of the different frog species were introduced in Chapter 3. As explained before, there is one species, the much-admired Motorbike Frog, that come spring and early summer, will be trying to lay their eggs in almost any body of standing water. Just try to keep them out of a pond! But because they do breed so readily, we know a lot about the breeding behaviour and preferences of Motorbike Frogs.

Unfortunately, the same cannot be said for many of our other local frog species, some of which are very fussy and as a result, poorly known. What follows then is our 'best guess' at the kind of pond conditions that might encourage each of the other frog species to breed.

Slender Tree Frogs appear to be fairly social animals, often grouping together even where they have space to spread out. As such, they may need a certain size pond to form a calling or breeding group. Through much of the year they climb tall sedges and rushes at dusk to feed on flying insects, but in spring they remain at water level to pair up and deposit the egg masses. These are laid about 10 cm below the water level, hence a breeding pond would need to be at least this deep. It may also need to contain tall emergent sedges or rushes such as the Lake Club-Sedge, *Schoenoplectus validus*, or the Broad Twig Sedge, *Baumea preissii*. At least part of the pool should probably be more than 30 cm deep, as Slender Tree Frog tadpoles often dive into the water column when disturbed.

Banjo Frogs often lay their 'foam raft' egg masses in quite shallow water (10-20 cm), but usually under cover of dense emergent or overhanging vegetation. They may favour larger ponds rather than small confined water bodies. Because Banjo Frog tadpoles take so long to develop and grow to such a large size, they probably need areas of deep water in a pond to avoid predators.

The various Froglets (Squelching, Bleating, Clicking and Quacking) all breed in very shallow water, usually no more than 10-20 cm. In a deep pond, this condition may be met by placing a container of soil and sedges on some bricks so that it sits just below the water level. Alternatively, it may be advisable to construct a special shallow pond or an overflow area from your main pond to accommodate these species. The tadpoles of all species also prefer shallow, sunlit water but with a layer of leaves or other debris for shelter.

Lea's Frog has the unusual habit of laying its eggs above the water, attached to overhanging vegetation. There is no obvious reason why it should not be able to do this around a garden pond, and we know of one garden where this appears to have happened. Because Lea's Frog lives mainly along well-shaded streams, it is likely that the tadpoles will do best in a deep, cool pond rather than a shallow, sunlit one.

Crawling Frogs might ideally breed in a special, purpose-built area that provides damp, litter strewn surfaces adjacent to a pond. Alternatively, they can be left to choose their own calling and egg-laying site in the garden. In this case, however, the eggs will need to be monitored closely and then transferred into a pond or containers after they hatch.

Turtle Frogs might be encouraged to breed in a very dry part of the garden. If natural breeding conditions are anything to go by, they would probably need a layer of natural litter under shrubs. The location of Turtle Frog breeding congregations appears to be relatively stable in natural bushland areas, hence the species may not relocate easily away from its traditional breeding sites. In any event, this would not be desirable or permissible unless the natural site was under direct threat of destruction.

Moaning Frogs would need very special circumstances to breed in a garden. This would have to involve an area of deep sand or soil that could be kept just lightly damp through summer but then flooded to overflow into a pond during winter. While this is not impossible, there could be no guarantee that the frogs would even dig their burrows in the designated place. Indeed, some evidence suggests that the male Moaning Frogs dig their burrows in pretty much the same spot year after year and thus may be very difficult to relocate.

Moaning Frog burrow with door open. The entrance may be sealed over during the day.

Ponds and bog gardens

Most of the breeding requirements for local frog species can probably be met through a combination of a conventional garden pond and what is often called a 'bog-garden'. The latter is essentially a pond that has been filled almost entirely with soil or other material, and which retains moisture through all or most of the year.

A bog garden more closely reproduces the kind of natural habitat occupied by many of our local frogs, especially the small ground frogs. However, unlike a traditional bog garden, your 'frog-bog' will need to include areas of shallow water through winter to accommodate egg-laying and tadpole development. This can be achieved either by using a drip-feed system or by setting up the bog garden to receive overflow from your main pond.

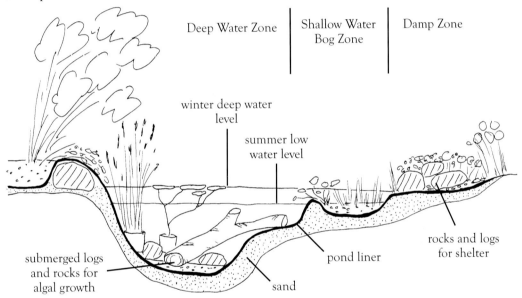

Deep Water Zone | Shallow Water Bog Zone | Damp Zone

winter deep water level

summer low water level

submerged logs and rocks for algal growth

sand

pond liner

rocks and logs for shelter

A general pond design incorporating both of these elements is shown above. However, this is only one of many possible variants on the same theme, and there is certainly no 'correct' way to set out your pond habitat. As explained below, there are also many different ways of constructing ponds and bog gardens, using a wide variety of different materials.

Choice of raw materials

There are various ways of constructing a pond, all of which basically involve digging a hole, then installing some kind of waterproof (impermeable) lining to hold water. In the past, most ponds were constructed from concrete, which was quite laborious and moderately expensive. Today, there are many options involving a diversity of materials and a wide range of costs and labour demands. A selection of these options are outlined below for your consideration.

The traditional concrete pond

These have largely gone out of favour over the last decade or so. We suspect that this is mainly because of the labour (and skill) required to build them and also because a concrete pond needs to stand for a month or so to allow the lime in the cement to leach out. Why wait for a month when you can have a pond and frogs tomorrow?

Concrete ponds also lack the flexibility offered by most other designs – they are permanent, immovable features that cannot be moved or easily modified to accommodate new design elements.

Prefabricated ponds made of moulded fibreglass or plastic

A wide variety of prefabricted designs are available from aquarium shops, irrigation businesses and general garden centres. They range in price from a few tens of dollars up to many hundreds, depending on size and complexity. A major advantage is that you can simply take them home, dig a hole and put them in the ground. Additionally, if it turns out that you have not installed the pond in the best possible spot in the garden, you can simply drain it, dig it up and move it. Too easy!

Some of the prefabricated ponds are quite well-designed to serve as frog ponds, with multiple levels to provide a range of water depths and some even with miniature waterfalls and cascades. Many of the larger and more elaborate ponds are designed to have the water circulating through a pump, and some are sold as a 'package' including a pump. Today, these pumps are usually very small, very quiet and quite cheap, and they draw comparatively little power. However, having a pump running does to some extent limit the types of ecological processes that might otherwise develop in your garden pond. In addition, some water plants such as lilies do not like circulating water. These are some of the things to consider when making your choice of pond designs and materials.

For many people, the major disadvantage of prefabricated ponds is the price, especially for the larger and more complex ponds. However, for some people the deciding factor may be a wish to have finer control of the design of the pond. This might be especially important if you are intending to try your hand at breeding some of the fussier species.

Ponds made from society's 'pre-loved' castoffs

Many perfectly serviceable ponds have been made from old bathtubs, laundry tubs, baby baths, children's paddling pools, horse troughs, old toilets .... the list could go on and on. The raw material for these ponds can usually be recycled from road-verge piles during 'council-cleanup' periods. For a really serious garden pond-builder, these periods can be quite magical!

All that is usually needed to turn an old bathtub or similar shaped container into a pond is to give them a very thorough scrubbing to remove any harmful residues, and to plug any outlet hole. After that, it is just a matter of choosing a spot and digging it in.

Ponds made from baths and sinks are often quite narrow and deep, and the pond water can remain quite cold, even through summer. The extra depth can also make them difficult to plant and maintain, hence it may be worthwhile placing a layer or two of old bricks in the

An attractive pond made from an old wash basin. Note the metal safety grid.

base of the pond to raise the base level. This platform will double as a maze of tunnels and passageways that will soon be occupied by a variety of creatures.

Ponds made with plastic liner

The development of heavy-duty, UV-resistant and chemical-free polyurethane plastic liner was a god-send to pond builders and frog lovers. It has allowed ponds to be constructed to very precise specifications, sometimes incorporating a combination of deep pools, shallow benches and overflow areas that will mirror the seasonal flooding of many of our natural wetlands. However, it can also be used in combination with other materials to design very simple and quick-to-build ponds. Various grades of liner are sold but we recommend that it be at least 0.5 mm thick, which should give a life of 20 years or more. Your local nursery or irrigation centre staff will be able to give more detailed advice about these products.

Tyre-ponds made from half of a car or truck tyre are a popular means of using plastic liner to create an instant and attractive pond. A simple design for a tyre pond is shown

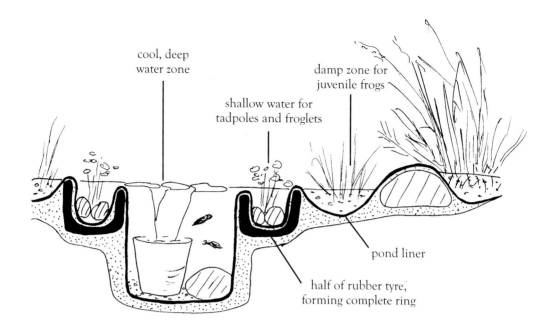

cool, deep
water zone

damp zone for
juvenile frogs

shallow water for
tadpoles and froglets

pond liner

half of rubber tyre,
forming complete ring

above. Another simple type of plastic liner pond uses the pine 'Easy-Edge' barricade that is sold as edging for garden beds. To make your Easy-Edge pond, simply join the edging strip into a closed shape of the desired size and shape, then cover the floor with a thick layer of newspapers or sacking, extending up over the barricade. By placing some bricks or similar beneath the paper, some variety of water depth can be achieved.

The next step is to enclose the whole structure with plastic liner, extending about 30 cm past the margin of the pond, and taking care to avoid any sharp wire or other projections on the Easy-Edge. The pond can then be filled, and any folds in the liner can be smoothed as the weight is taken up. Once the pond is nearly full, the edges can be folded over and held in place with small tacks or by gluing the liner to itself along folds. At several places around the margin of the pond, it will be necessary to build up a 'ramp' of rocks or bricks that will allow frogs to make their way into and out of the pond.

An advantage of this kind of pond is that it can be constructed on hard surfaces such as brick-paving or a concrete slab. However, in such a location it will be necessary to make sure that there are suitable feeding and sheltering spots nearby, and that the frogs will be able to make their way between these areas and the pond.

Plastic liner is also ideal for installing a pond at ground level. The first step is to set up a spirit-level and string and do some 'bush surveying' to make sure that water will sit and flow where you want it to. When you get to digging out the required shape, take the hole down a little deeper than you intend for the final pond. The extra depth will allow you to line the hole either with clean builders' sand or with a thick layer of newspaper, sacking or natural-fibre carpet. This precaution may stop the liner from getting punctured by a tree root or rock as the weight of the water starts to bear down.

The liner should extend about 30 cm past the edge of the hole, allowing it to be raised up above the high-water level. Rocks, railway sleepers or other pieces of timber should be gathered nearby as a means of anchoring down the margin of the line, but these should not be set in place until after the pond is filled. As this is happening, the pond liner should be adjusted to keep it as smooth as possible. Once the pond is full, it is then time to bed down the margins, making use of the rocks, logs and soil to form a complex and secure 'pond-margin' that will hopefully provide food, shelter and a place to meet other frogs.

Other useful hints in pond design and construction

There are a number of other points that should be kept in mind when constructing all kinds of garden ponds. In no particular order:

- Consider raising the pond surface slightly above that of the general garden. This will reduce the risk of surface flow carrying unwanted nutrients into the pond.

- Take care not to dig straight through the telephone cable. We won't be saying who has done that before!

- For large ponds, consider installing a drainage system, perhaps connected through to a soak-well or sewage pipe. This can be extremely useful in the event that you need to empty the pond for maintenance.

Is a water-pump or aerator necessary?

In your ecologically balanced pond, the addition of a pump or artificial aerator will be a matter of choice and not a necessity. Plenty of oxygen will be available through controlling the nutrient input and from water plants submerged in the pond.

There are a number of reasons why you might decide to install a pump or filtering system for your pond. Apart from increasing oxygen and ensuring good water clarity, a pump will let you add miniature rapids, a rocky creek bed or a waterfall to your pond setting. It may also come in handy if you wish to drain the pond. The pump should have a sponge type foam filter so that tadpoles and other pond life will not get sucked in; alternatively, place the intake pipe where it is not accessible to tadpoles. It may be necessary to build a mesh enclosure to house any parts that could cause problems. Some plants such as water-lilies need still water to grow, so these will need to be kept well away from the pump.

Pond maintenance

If your pond has been designed and positioned well, it should be virtually maintenance-free. During summer it will probably be necessary to top up the water level in a deep pond, while at the same time allowing the bog garden to dry out naturally. This water can be taken straight from the hose, provided that any hot water is flushed through first. It is also important that the volume of new water added does not exceed 5% of the total volume in any one day.

The only other real maintenance issues concern the cleaning out of excess, decomposing leaf-fall, as already discussed earlier, and the occasional pruning or culling of the more aggressive water and fringing plants. One experienced pond-builder has recommended a once-yearly prune and general clean-out of all ponds, and has reported better breeding success after this treatment. The best time of year to do this is probably late autumn, after all or most tadpoles have emerged, and at a time when growth of plants has slowed.

A final point on this topic of pond maintenance is that any water drained from your frog ponds should ideally be disposed of in your own garden, rather than flushed into the storm-water system. There are two reasons for this. First, the water is too precious to just flush it away. If possible it should be poured into litter beds or deep sheltering areas that harbour Moaning or Banjo Frogs. And second, the water might be carrying zoospores of the chytrid fungus, and so should not be allowed to enter the storm-water system – most of that water ends up going into Perth's major wetlands.

Pond safety

Pond safety is a very important issue. With swimming pools we have very strict rules concerning fencing and access for young children. The same rules do not seem to apply for garden ponds, presumably because it is not intended that any child would deliberately enter a fish or frog pond. Nevertheless, garden ponds obviously do pose a threat to children, especially the very young, and we do need to be responsible in our design and construction.

Probably the best safeguard against accidents is to install a metal mesh either just above or just under the water surface. This will double as a safety grill and as a place where frogs will perch to bask in the sun. It will not interfere with egg-laying or with tadpole activity and will supply a peace of mind that is worth any loss of aesthetic quality in the pond.

For a very large pond, it may not be possible to install a grid over the entire surface. In such a case, you may need to enclose the pond within a locked fence, at least while there is any possibility of a young child falling in. For older children, a wide, shallow pond with water plants in pots is unlikely to pose any real threat. Even so, someone will probably still fall in, sooner or later!

Spotted-thighed Frog, a relative of the Motorbike Frog, found east of Albany.

CHAPTER 6:

Bringing Your Pond to Life

Now comes the real fun! Starting with a bare pond or bog garden, it is now time to turn it into a living, healthy ecosystem. But don't expect everything to happen overnight. Many of the plants and animals will take a little time to settle into their new home and perhaps even longer to begin functioning as a complete ecosystem.

Sources of water

Water for the ponds would ideally come from a rain water tank, in which case only a day or two's delay would be necessary before the pond could be stocked with plants and wild creatures.

If no rainwater is available, scheme water from a garden tap and hose can be used to fill the pond. However, this contains significant quantities of dissolved chemicals including chlorine, that are deadly to tadpoles. To eliminate the chlorine, tap water should be left standing in the sun for a full week prior to introducing any live plants or animals.

Plants for the pond and its surrounds

Selecting the right plants to include in and around your pond can be a daunting prospect, if only because of the sheer variety of choice. Success in pond planting is rarely achieved through use of any particular plant species, but rather from using a balanced mixture of plant types of various growth forms and heights.

The lists of plants given below is adapted from the 'Perth Plants' series mentioned earlier. It is intended as a general guideline only. Your particular choice of plant should be governed by soil types, topography, available space, climate, personal preference and availability of the plants. The staff of your local Nursery will be able to advise on the most suitable plants for your location. Associations such as *Greening Western Australia, Apace Western Australia* and the *Wildflower Society* can offer advice on gardening with local native plants.

Submergent Plants

Otherwise known as water plants, these provide food and shelter for aquatic fauna. They also take up nutrients during their growth and put oxygen back into the water. No more than a quarter of the surface area of the pond should be covered with floating vegetation, as this can restrict gas exchange and cause the water to stagnate.

Any plants that will have their roots in or directly adjacent the pond are best grown in submerged pots or in bags made of shade-cloth. In either case, the new plants should be repotted into relatively clean sand so as to minimise leaching of nutrients into the pond. By keeping the various submergent and emergent plants in separate containers, it is possible to quickly empty any part of the pond for maintenance, and also much easier to control the growth of any particular plant.

There are only a few local native water plants. Two of these are listed below.

Ottelia ovalifolia (Native Waterlily)
Triglochin procera (Water Ribbons)

Many other kinds of water plants are on sale through nurseries and aquarium shops. Some of these are native Australian plants, but many more are exotics. Some of the exotics grow very quickly and will need to be culled regularly. Indeed, a few are so aggressive that they have become aquatic weeds in our local waterways. A number of these are banned throughout Western Australia and should be reported to Agriculture WA if seen. They are illustrated in Weednote No. 1/97, available from Agriculture WA. As a general safety precaution, no pond plant should ever be released into a natural waterway or swamp.

Emergent Plants

These are plants that have their roots in water or in waterlogged soil, but have much of their stems and leaves out of the water. The best known group in this category are the rushes and sedges. Some of these are best grown standing in the pond, while others prefer to be planted around the margin or in an associated bog garden. They provide excellent feeding and breeding habitat for small ground frogs and Slender Tree Frogs. Some local native emergent plants are:

Baumea preissii (Broad Twig Rushes)
Juncus pallidus (Pale Rushes)
Carex fasicicularis (Tassel Sedge)

Tassel Sedge

Lepidosperma longitudinale (Pithy Sword-Sedge)
Isolepis nodosa (Knotted Club Rush)
Schoenoplectus validus (Lake Club-Rush)

Groundcovers

Groundcovers help discourage weed growth, they retain soil moisture and can reduce erosion in sloping areas. They provide shelter and protection from predators for frogs on the move. Clicking Froglets will breed inside a dense cover of plants such as *Centella* or *Dichondra*, provided the ground surface remains saturated through winter. Local native groundcovers include:

Conostylis setigera (Bristly Cottonheads)
Dampiera linearis (Common Linearis)
Pattersonia occidentalis (Purple Flag)
Pimelea ferruginea (Coast Banjine)
Lobelia alata (Ribbed Lobelia)
Dichondra repens (Kidney Grass)
Centella species (Centella)
Scaevola crassifolia (Thick-Leaved Fan Flower)

Centella

Climbers and Creepers

These plants not only look attractive hanging over the edge of your pond, but they can also aid in the movement of small frogs getting in and out of the water. Motorbike Frogs and Banjo Frogs will call from beneath the overhanging vegetation and may even lay their eggs and foam rafts in such places. A selection of local native climbers and creepers follow:

Hardenbergia comptoniana (Native Wisteria)
Kennedia coccinea (Coral Vine)
Kennedia prostrata (Running Postman)
Clematis linearifolia (Old Man's Beard)

Small to medium shrubs

Some varieties of native shrubs are small enough to provide groundcover, while others grow to heights that provide a shady canopy. Many species such as the Acacias are particularly attractive to many types of frog insect prey. Prickly Moses (*Acacia pulchella*) is a good choice where access needs to be discouraged, either for cats and dogs or for small children. As its name suggests, it can form a very effective barrier, but without restricting the movement of frogs. Other local natives include:

Bossiaea eriocarpa (Common Brown Pea)
Hypocalymma angustifolim (White Myrtle)
Acacia drummondii (Drummond's Wattle)
Adenanthos cygnorum (Woolly Bush)
Beaufortia squarrosa (Sand Bottlebrush)
Calothamnus lateralis (Swamp Blood Flower)
Astartea fascicularis (Pink Flowered Astartea)

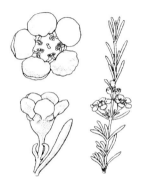

Pink Flowered Astartea

Larger shrubs and trees

The larger shrubs and trees listed below provide excellent shade canopy and produce modest amounts of slow-decomposing leaf fall. Many of the myrtaceous plants such as the Eucalypts and Paperbarks also support diverse bird and insect communities when in flower.

Eucalyptus marginata (Jarrah)
Melaleauca rhaphiophylla (Swamp Paperbark)
Agonis linearifolia (Swamp Peppermint)
Viminaria juncea (Golden Spray)
Jacksonia furcellata (Grey Stinkwood)
Oxylobium lineare (Swan River Pea)

Fruit

Swamp Paperbark

Aquatic Invertebrates

In time, your garden pond will become a home for a myriad of fascinating aquatic invertebrates. The bigger ones will include mayflies, caddisflies, damselflies, water spiders, backswimmers and water-boatmen; and all of their aquatic larvae. An even greater variety awaits a closer look with a hand-lens or microscope – water fleas, seed shrimps, water mites and many more.

Many of these creatures will make their own way into your pond as flying adults or as larvae or eggs on the legs and feathers of waterbirds. However, it is possible to get things started by taking a few jars of water from a nearby artificial wetland or even from a roadside ditch. This will contain a host of tiny creatures that can form the start of your own pond life. Be extra careful not to introduce any Mosquito Fish (*Gambusia*; see below) into the pond in this way.

The variety of life in every pond will be slightly different, as it depends on a number of factors such as oxygen and nutrient content, temperature and the age and location of a particular pond. In general, however, the more established and the healthier your pond, the more diverse the aquatic life will be. If you are interested in discovering more about the aquatic life of your pond, there is an excellent book by Jenny Davis and Faye Christidis (see under Other Resources) and various additional fact sheets produced by organisations such as the Water and Rivers Commission.

Before leaving this topic, it is worth restating the fact that many of these pond invertebrates, most notably the dragonfly larvae and water beetles, are significant predators on frog eggs and tadpoles. This is not to say that they represent the enemy in a frog breeding pond. In reality, the consumption of tadpoles by other pond life is a perfectly natural part of pond ecology and it should not affect the breeding success of your frogs.

To understand why tadpoles must get eaten, it is good to remember that females of most

Larvae of dragonfly (left) and damselfly (right).

local frog species lay many hundreds or even thousands of eggs at a time. Clearly, not all of these are expected to survive. Indeed, some individual animals, such as a Banjo Frog female, might lay upwards of 50,000 eggs in her lifetime. Just imagine what the world would be like if even 1% of them survived, followed by 1% of each of their offspring, and so on. In no time at all, the world would be covered in a thick layer of Banjo Frogs!

From another perspective, all of those extra eggs and tadpoles provide a huge quantity of available protein for a great many other creatures – creatures that in turn walk or fly away to play other important roles in the wider ecosystem. Viewed in this way, frogs along with their huge quantities of eggs and tadpoles, are clearly of great importance in the wetland and bushland ecosystems. Even more reason why we should be trying our hardest to conserve not only the rare frogs, but the common ones too.

Fish

Fish can be an excellent addition to a garden pond. As noted earlier, they can be used as one part of a broader strategy to control mosquitoes in your garden. They will also help to maintain a natural balance in the general invertebrate community. But can fish and frogs coexist in a garden pond?

Special mention was made earlier of the Mosquito Fish or Gambusia (*Gambusia affinis*). This species is native to the rivers that drain into the Gulf of Mexico, but has been introduced to many parts of the world as a means of controlling mosquitoes. As a mosquito control, Gambusia has been a miserable failure. However, in many countries including Australia, it has managed to adapt to local conditions and in the process has wreaked havoc upon native fish and aquatic life generally. The main secret to its success is a remarkable ability to breed, with only a few fish capable of multiplying up into millions within a single season.

In feeding trials, Gambusia appear to be reluctant to eat the eggs or tadpoles of local frogs. Nevertheless, in places where Gambusia reaches plague proportions, the swarming fish will damage and kill tadpoles in large numbers. This might easily happen in a garden pond, where Gambusia populations would soon run out of their preferred food items and lead them to other targets including tadpoles.

10 mm

Gambusia

Another inhabitant of many garden ponds is the common goldfish. These are known to eat frogs' eggs and the early tadpole stages, but they generally will not harm larger tadpoles. Goldfish are not capable of such prolific breeding activity as Gambusia and so do not pose anything like the same threat to your pond ecosystem.

There are various small local native fishes that appear to be well-suited to life in a garden pond. All of them will probably eat a few frogs' eggs and the very tiny stage tadpoles but, like the goldfish, they breed quite slowly and so are incapable of doing any real harm to a population of tadpoles.

Some local native fish species are the Western Pygmy Perch (*Edelia vittata*), the Western Minnow (*Galaxias occidentalis*) and the Swan River Goby (*Pseudogobius olorum*). These all appear to be fairly effective at controlling mosquitoes and all are well adapted to Western Australian conditions.

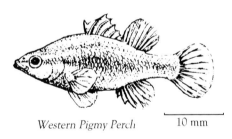

Western Pigmy Perch   10 mm

All three species are available at least occasionally through the specialist aquarium shops, with signs that the Western Pygmy Perch may soon be more readily available. The more that people ask for these fishes, the more likely the shops are to stock them.

Other native fish that seem to do quite well alongside tadpoles in garden ponds are the Spotted Minnow (*Galaxias maculatus*), a native of our south coastal streams, and the Pacific Blue-Eye (*Pseudomugil signifer*), a native of eastern Australia. One exotic fish that is freely available commercially is the White Cloud Mountain Minnow (*Tanichthys albonubes*), a native of southeast Asia.

For a small pond, an initial population of two or three fish is probably adequate for mosquito control. These may breed in your pond, but only to a point where the numbers are in balance with the productivity of the pond.

Frogs and tadpoles

Frogs seem to be able to sense a cool, inviting pond from quite far away. This means that they will probably turn up sooner or later under their own steam to occupy your frog-friendly garden. However, in many areas, frog populations are now so patchy and depleted that this may take years, perhaps even decades.

Frog conservationists are divided over whether frogs should ever be moved from one place to another. The main concerns are with mixing up distinct genetic stock, spreading infectious diseases, and introducing frogs into inappropriate environments. All of these are valid concerns, especially where frogs are going to be moved any great distance.

We take the view that that the frog crisis is sufficiently serious to warrant a small amount of positive human intervention. This should be focussed on rebuilding population numbers, on recolonising of new habitats, and on establishing contact between isolated populations, especially in the major metropolitan centres. Nevertheless, there are two golden rules that must be followed without exception when moving frogs, frog eggs or tadpoles.

The first is that frogs or tadpoles should never be removed from, or released into a natural wetland including streams or brooks. Rather, frogs or tadpoles should only ever be taken from one of the following contexts

- From a locality near to your home where they are under immediate threat of destruction – for example, eggs or tadpoles that have been laid in someone's swimming pool or in a temporary roadside puddle; or frogs and tadpoles in a nearby area that is about to be cleared for development.

- From a nearby frog-friendly garden that has an excess of tadpoles (Adult frogs moved under these circumstances will probably just go back to their former home)

So what constitutes 'nearby'. Again it helps to think like a frog!

The main guiding principle is to stay within the range of natural movements of the frogs themselves. In the case of the larger frogs, this means that eggs or tadpoles can be moved over distances of at least 5 km without having any adverse impact on genetic structure or on the wider distribution of the frog fungus disease. For the smaller frogs, such as the various froglet species, the individual distances moved are obviously much smaller. However, we know from genetic studies that even these tiny froglets have essentially the same genetic makeup over quite large distances of 10s to 100s of kilometres. A 'frog rescue' distance of less than 3 km is probably a good one to adhere to for these smaller frogs.

The second golden rule is that frogs, tadpoles or eggs must not be moved between localities on the coastal plain and in the Darling Range; and *vice versa*. The reason for this is that each of these areas has a number of unique species that might cause problems of interbreeding if introduced into the other environment.

In the Alcoa Frog Watch office at the Western Australian Museum, we try to assist the process of frog and tadpole rescue by putting people who are looking for some tadpoles to add to a garden pond in touch with people who are trying to get rid of unwanted or excess tadpoles. This service avoids the distasteful alternative of having to destroy tadpoles where they have been laid in a swimming pool or other inconvenient location. We call this is our Tadpole Rescue and Exchange, and invite you to make use of this service. For obvious reasons, we are not in a position to supply tadpoles ourselves. However, we may well be able to help you locate some that will otherwise have met with a sad end.

Until quite recently, tadpoles of the Motorbike Frog were available from pet shops, but only ever for use as live fish food. This trade was stopped when we first became aware of the presence of the frog fungus disease in Western Australia, on the grounds that it posed an obvious risk of further spreading the disease. It has not been resumed.

If you are in any doubt about the appropriateness of rescuing and relocating frogs or tadpoles from any particular locality, please don't hesitate to contact us at Alcoa Frog Watch. Anyone wishing to relocate tadpoles into a natural wetland habitat will need to contact the *Department of Conservation and Land Management.*

Managing the spread of frog fungus disease

Every time you bring any frogs or tadpoles into your garden from another locality, you are running the risk of introducing the frog fungus disease. The same applies for bringing in wetlands plants from a plant nursery or a water sample containing invertebrates or fish. Naturally, the reverse applies for moving any animals, plants or water from your garden to other localities.

The chytrid fungus is spread by tiny zoospores that can probably survive for several days or longer as free-swimming organisms. These are easily transported and cannot be eradicated at present without the fungicide also killing a range of other, beneficial organisms (including an infected frog).

Given the ease with which the frog fungus has spread, and the fact that infected frogs are themselves capable of moving over considerable distances, there seems little prospect of ever maintaining your garden as a 'fungus-free' zone. Sooner or later, the frog fungus is bound to get in, either with a visiting frog or perhaps on the damp feet of a visiting waterbird.

Faced with this situation, we feel that the best approach is for everyone to focus their efforts on keeping the individual frogs in good, general health and in building up their garden frog population to a level where it can survive a fungal epidemic.

As indicated already, garden frogs or tadpoles should not be released into a natural wetland habitat without first getting permission from the *Department of Conservation and Land Management*.

Eggs of Lea's Frog suspended above a stream.

CHAPTER 7:

BREEDING FROGS IN YOUR GARDEN!

Once you have frogs living in your garden it should only be a matter of time before they start to breed. In most cases, there is nothing else that you will need to do, except sit back and enjoy the miracle of frog reproduction. However, in some circumstances you may need to intervene in small ways to overcome specific problems.

Caring for eggs

There are really only two circumstances where you might need to give frog eggs any extra help. The first is if your frogs share a pond with a goldfish or some other egg-hungry fish species. This problem can be circumvented either by removing the fish for a period, or by transferring the tadpoles to a container until they grow to a safe size.

Eggs of a Moaning Frog, prior to hatching in a burrow.

You can experiment a little to see what size tadpole is safe from your particular fish. Remember to use rain water in the container, or allow tap water to stand for a week in the sun before introducing the eggs or tadpoles.

The other circumstance is where clutches of Moaning Frog eggs have been laid in garden burrows. The burrows should be carefully excavated a few weeks after the cessation of calling, and any contained tadpoles moved across into your pond (or into a safe container if they are still small and vulnerable to fish hunger). This process has the same effect as natural flooding of the burrow and release of the tadpoles into a stream or swamp. It may help to mark the burrow entrances while the males are still calling. A similar process may be needed in the event that Crawling Frogs lay eggs away from a pond, but their eggs and tadpoles are much easier to locate.

Rearing tadpoles

Tadpoles are also quite capable of looking after themselves. However, just as a frog-friendly garden has a *carrying capacity* in terms of the number of frogs that it can feed and shelter, so too does a pond when it comes to tadpoles.

For a garden pond, the carrying capacity is determined partly by the amount of food and shelter, but also by the extent of crowding of the tadpoles. As with frogs, supplementary food can be provided to reduce loss of tadpoles through starvation, and additional shelter can be provided by adding extra logs or rocks into the pond. Not much can be done about the problem of overcrowding in a small pond. This has the effect of reducing the growth rate of the tadpoles, even when food is abundant.

For a small pond such as one made from a car tyre, a realistic survival rate out of an initial clutch of 2000 eggs is probably only a few dozen tadpoles getting through to juvenile frogs. With the provision of extra food, this may rise to perhaps 50-100 young frogs.

Supplementary feeding of tadpoles is quite straightforward, but it is also easy to get overenthusiastic about it. A good food supplement is made by boiling well-rinsed lettuce or spinach leaves (taking care to remove any remnant pesticides; organic grown is even safer) for

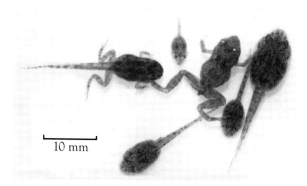

10 mm

Tadpoles of a Squelching Froglet, showing various stages of development.

about 20 minutes until it turns paste-like. It can then be drained, cooled and pressed into small pellets that can be frozen for future use. The white flesh of zucchinis can be used instead of green-leafed vegetables.

Vegetable pellets should only be added to a pond or container if the tadpoles show immediate interest in eating them. If they are not eaten, it generally means that the tadpoles are already getting enough natural algae and are not hungry. Any pellets that are not fully consumed should be removed before they start to decompose and foul the water.

Fish flakes and dry dog food are also commonly used as a food supplement for tadpoles. These should be used sparingly and once again, only if the tadpoles are obviously interested in them.

A better way of increasing the survival rate from a clutch is to divide the tadpoles between a number of separate rearing containers. These can be almost any size and shape, but should be set up to closely mirror the conditions in the pond. They should contain some floating or emergent plants to provide oxygen, some submerged rocks or logs for algal growth, and a combination of partial sunlight and shade through the day. As the tadpoles begin to develop into frogs, they should be given places to cling, and later, a means of climbing out of the container. A piece of shade cloth draped into the water is an ideal means of escape.

Occasionally, tadpoles seem not to want to turn into frogs, even after many months of development. This often seems to happen with clutches of Motorbike Frogs eggs that have been laid quite late in the season. What seems to be going on is that these late tadpoles miss whatever it is that triggers the normal process of conversion into frogs, and hence they get left behind as tadpoles. In some cases, they can be given a hurry along by placing them in shallow water, to simulate the effect of a pond drying up. If this fails, then it's probably best to just leave them alone - they will more than likely turn into frogs early in the next breeding season.

Caring for juvenile frogs

The first few weeks or month of a juvenile frog's life is a particularly dangerous time. Not only is it a time when many young frogs succumb to the effects of the chytrid fungus disease, but it is also a period when they are especially prone to both predation and death by dehydration.

A young frog is in some ways still quite like a tadpole. This is especially true of their skin that takes several weeks or longer to mature into the thicker and less permeable covering of the adult frog. During this period, the young frogs are reluctant to leave the moist areas immediately around the margin of a pond. As a result, they are easy pickings for many predators that know precisely where to look for them. For example, ravens and other equally-intelligent, predatory birds are often seen moving along the margin of a wetland in spring, systematically eating their way through groups of newly-emerged frogs.

Juvenile frogs have a fair chance of survival if your pond is bordered by a zone of dense ground cover plants, giving them plenty of moist habitat in which to hide. This can be further improved by building a special shelter (such as a low pile of loosely stacked tiles or bricks) for the juvenile frogs to occupy close to the margin of the pond.

Another way of giving them a better chance of survival is to place some chicken wire or other mesh over the pond and its surrounds through the critical month or so after the young frogs first start to emerge. This will not stop predation by spiders, centipedes etc, but it might well defeat that one ibis or raven that might otherwise wipe out your population.

Juvenile Banjo Frog. Note the characteristically large head of young frog.

Looking after injured and sick frogs

With a large and diverse frog community living in your garden, you may occasionally come across injured and sick frogs. Injuries can occur as a result of attacks by predatory birds or other animals, or by accidental crushing.

In such instances there may be little that you can do to help the injured frog, other than to bring it into temporary captivity while it goes about healing the injury itself.

Fortunately, frogs are not without considerable defenses of their own, including a suite of powerful on-board antibiotic chemicals contained within their skin. The power of frogs to heal wounds is clearly seen from the incidence of scars and other healed wounds on many larger, older frogs. Remember too that frogs have the remarkable ability to regrow parts of limbs in the event of loss, provided they do not get finished off by another predator whilst in the process of recovery.

Very badly injured frogs can be euthanased humanely by placing them into a freezer inside a bag or other container, or they can be taken to a vet to be put down.

A frog can be maintained inside in an aquarium or other suitable container while it attempts to mend its injuries. This should be put in a place that receives some natural sunlight but does not catch the full heat of the day, and it should contain a place for the frog to hide. Obviously, it must be kept moist at all times and frog food should be added regularly, either by catching and introducing live prey items, or by adding a handful of invertebrate-rich leaf litter every few days (your garden should have plenty of that by now). Keep in mind that a frog can drown if the water level is too high in an aquarium.

If your injured frog survives but is disabled and unlikely to make it back in the wide world, then you may choose to keep it inside permanently. To do so, you may need to obtain a wildlife keeper's licence from the *Department of Conservation and Land Management.* You should contact staff of their Wildlife Branch and discuss your situation. Under current legislation, you do not need a licence whilst caring for a sick or injured native animal.

There are various books on captive maintenance of amphibians, mostly written overseas but still quite useful. Some of these are listed at the end of this booklet.

Little is yet known about the diseases of frogs. The chytrid fungus disease mentioned earlier produces symptoms of lethargy and unusual behaviour including sitting out in full sun and failing to properly retract the legs. Unfortunately, by the time a frog starts to show these kinds of symptoms, it is probably within a day or two of death. With animals in obvious distress you may wish to employ euthanasia rather than have them linger and suffer.

One kind of frog behaviour that is sometimes misinterpreted as a symptom of disease is a strange gulping action, often accompanied by use of the forelimb to wipe the body or face. If you watch this behaviour carefully, you may see small rolls of loose skin being drawn towards the corner of the mouth and eventually eaten. This is a normal process whereby the outer layer of skin is being renewed and the slough consumed making use of the protein. It is normally finished within 10-15 minutes.

CHAPTER 8:

SHARING THE SECRETS OF YOUR SUCCESS

As you might have picked up by reading this booklet, the process of building a frog-friendly garden contains a significant element of trial and error, of experimenting with different pond and garden designs, and perhaps even of luck and chance discovery. For many of the local species, we really do not know what conditions will encourage animals to visit or breed in your garden, for the simple reason that no one has ever done it before.

Alcoa Frog Watch provides an opportunity for everyone to share their successes or failures with the rest of the frog-loving community. Through our newsletters and website, we are able to effectively disseminate and share information on improved designs for ponds, bog gardens, and feeding or sheltering stations, so that we can all benefit from each other's experiences.

One way that you can help is by completing the Garden Frog Survey that will be distributed several times a year from now on with the Alcoa Frog Watch newsletter. This will ask you to provide a brief summary of what you have done to make your garden more frog-friendly over the survey period, and what your frogs have done in response. Have you seen any new species turn up in your garden? Have any of them been calling or laid any eggs? Have you seen juveniles of any species? And so on.

To help us gather and share good, reliable information, we would encourage you to maintain a simple diary of your efforts and achievements in *Building Frog Friendly Gardens*. This will remove any uncertainty about times and numbers when it comes to filling in your survey forms, and it may also grow into a wonderful record of your activities that could well be cherished by your children, grandchildren, and generations to come.

Apart from the survey, we will always welcome letters, emails or phone calls from anyone who feels that they made a breakthrough in some area of *Building Frog Friendly Gardens*. Don't be afraid to share your observations or news, even if it might seem a bit peculiar or unlikely. Just remember that most of humanity's best ideas have seemed a bit wacky at the time!

Good luck and enjoy your frogs!

OTHER USEFUL RESOURCES

Books and leaflets

'A Guide to Wetland Invertebrates of southwestern Australia' by J. Davis and F. Christidis. Western Australian Museum, Perth, Western Australia. 1997. 177 pp.

'Attracting frogs to your garden' by K. Casey. Kimberley Publications, Upper Mount Gravatt, Queensland. 1996. 136 pp.

'Frogs as pets: a guide to keeping the Australian Green Tree Frog (*Litoria caerulea*)' by M. J. Tyler. Graphic Print Group, Adelaide.

'Frogs of Western Australia' by M. Tyler, L. A. Smith and R. E. Johnstone. Western Australian Museum, Perth, Western Australia. 3rd Edition. 2000. 194 pp.

'Frogs, Toads, and Treefrogs. A Complete Pet Owner's Manual' by R. D. Bartlett and P. P. Bartlett. Barron's Educational Series, Hauppauge, New York. 104 pp.

'Growing Locals – Gardening with local plants in Perth' by R. Powell and J. Emberson. West Australian Naturalists' Club Inc., Perth, Western Australia. 1996.

'Native vegetation of freshwater rivers & creeks in south Western Australia' by L. Chalmers and J. Wheeler. Waters and Rivers Commission, East Perth, Western Australia. 1997. 44 pp.

'Perth Plants for your garden' compiled by D. Crosbie. Greening Western Australia, Perth, Western Australia. 1996. 91 pp.

'Serious aquatic weeds of Western Australia'. Weednote No. 1/97. Agriculture Western Australia. 1997. 4 pp.

Websites

Alcoa Frog Watch: www.museum.wa.gov.au/frogwatch

Amphibian Diseases Website: www.jcu.edu.au/school/phtm/PHTM/frogs/ampdis.htm

Swan River Trust: www.wrc.wa.gov.au/srt

Waters and Rivers Commission: www.wrc.wa.gov.au